The prisoner who freed others

Acts 27—28 FOR CHILDREN

Written by Mervin Marquardt

Illustrated by Obata Designs, Alice Hausner

ARCH Books

COPYRIGHT © 1974 CONCORDIA PUBLISHING HOUSE, ST. LOUIS, MISSOURI
CONCORDIA PUBLISHING HOUSE LTD., LONDON, E. C. 1
MANUFACTURED IN THE UNITED STATES OF AMERICA
ALL RIGHTS RESERVED
ISBN 0-570-06081-8

Julie was taking her very first trip
Away from her home and alone.
Grabbing her suitcase, she boarded a ship
With people all going to Rome.

But Julie was lonely
 and wanted a friend,
So she looked
 at the people a while:
Quiet ones, noisy ones,
 busy ones too—
She hoped she would see
 someone smile.

Then off in a corner she spotted a face,
The happiest face she could see.
The man was a prisoner, Julie could tell,
But somehow he seemed to be free.

With hope in her eyes Julie sat down by him
And gave a small tug at his coat.
"Hello, little girl," the prisoner said.
"Could I be your friend on this boat?"

"Mister, oh, would you?" said Julie with glee,
And quickly asked, "What is your name?
Why are you wearing those nasty old chains?
A nice man like you! What a shame!"

Gently he answered, "My first name is Paul,
And I am God's servant, you see.
A few weeks ago I was preaching His love,
But some people grew angry with me.

"They started a riot, and I was arrested
And thrown into jail a while.
Although I am Jewish, I'm also a Roman,
So I'm going to Rome for my trial."

None of this mattered to Julie at all;
Paul's freedom was all she could see.
Joking and playing some games with her friend,
The days were as nice as could be.

Julie was happy when finally they reached
The first stop along the long trip:
A place called Safe Harbors on the island of Crete,
A rest for the people on ship.

But Jason the captain said, "Sorry to say,
The first winter storm soon will start.
I know of a city nearby where we'll stay,
So winter won't blow us apart."

Then Jason set sail for a short one-day trip.
But before very much time had passed,
A fierce winter storm shook the boat from the stern
Right up to the tip of the mast.

The waves soon were splashing all over the boat
And almost swept Julie from sight.
She nearly fell over the side of the ship,
But the prisoner Paul held her tight.

For many days Julie and all on the ship
Thought soon everybody would die.
The darkening clouds and rains were so thick
That the people could not see the sky.

Jason was frightened; but prisoner Paul
Said in a voice free of fear,
"Don't be afraid. God will keep us from harm.
He's promised; His angels are near."

Then all of a sudden one midnight a voice
Called loudly, "Hey! Land must be near!
An hour ago the ocean was deep,
But the water is shallow right here."

And as the sun rose, the shore came in sight.
Jason said, "Just like I planned.
All right, everybody, hang on very tight!
No doubt we will make it to land."

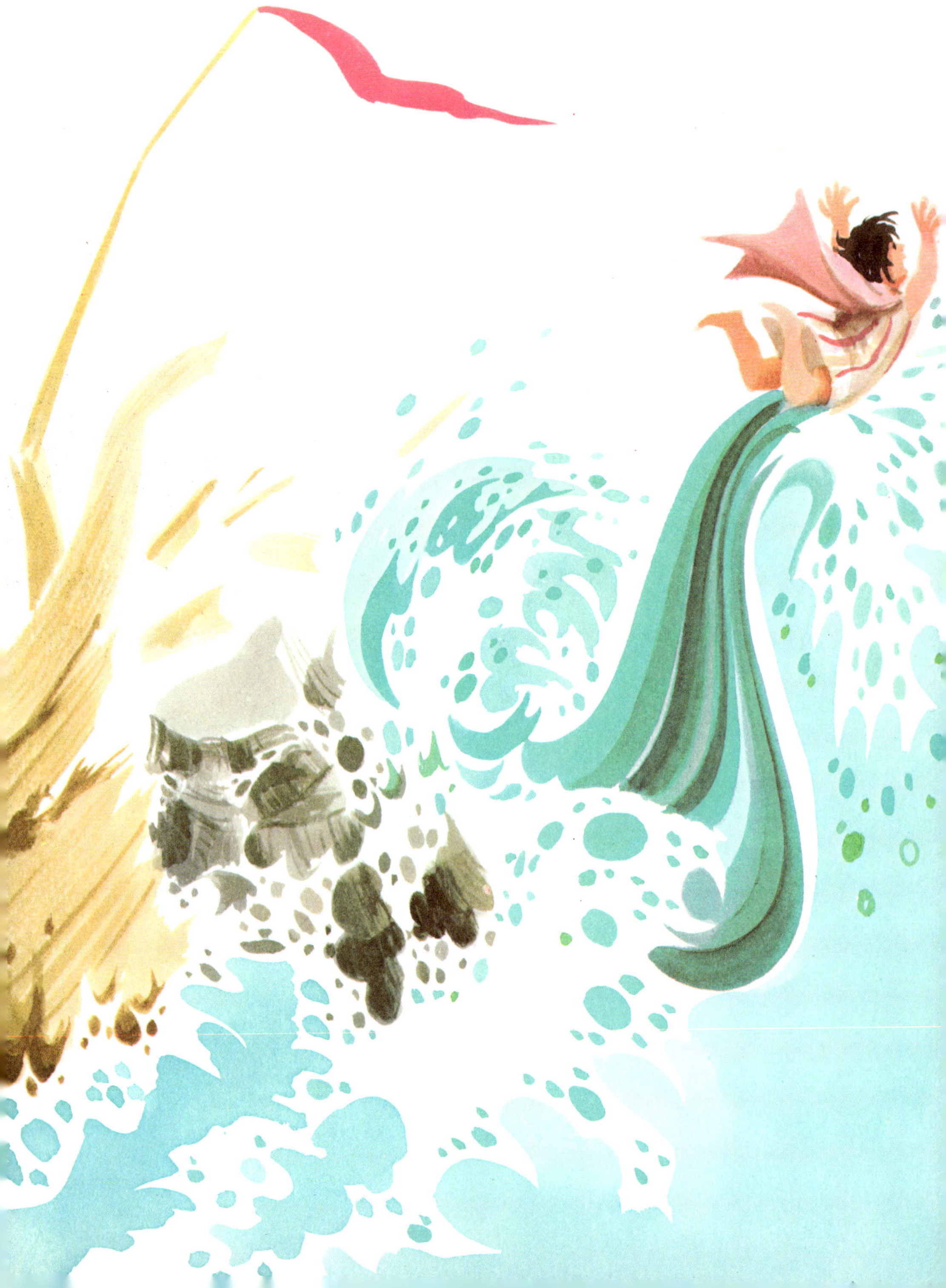

Faster and faster they sped toward the land
As the people were shouting with glee.
When, BANG! SCRAPE! GROAN! CRASH!
The ship hit a rock in the sea.

Suddenly Julie fell right off the boat;
A friendly wave gave her a hand.
On shore she saw all of her passenger friends.
They all had come safely to land.

People who lived there came running to help
The injured who lay on the shore,
To bandage their bruises and make a big fire,
To dry the wet clothes that they wore.

Julie saw Paul taking care of the people
And moving them close to the fire
And gathering branches to add to the fuel,
To help everybody get drier.

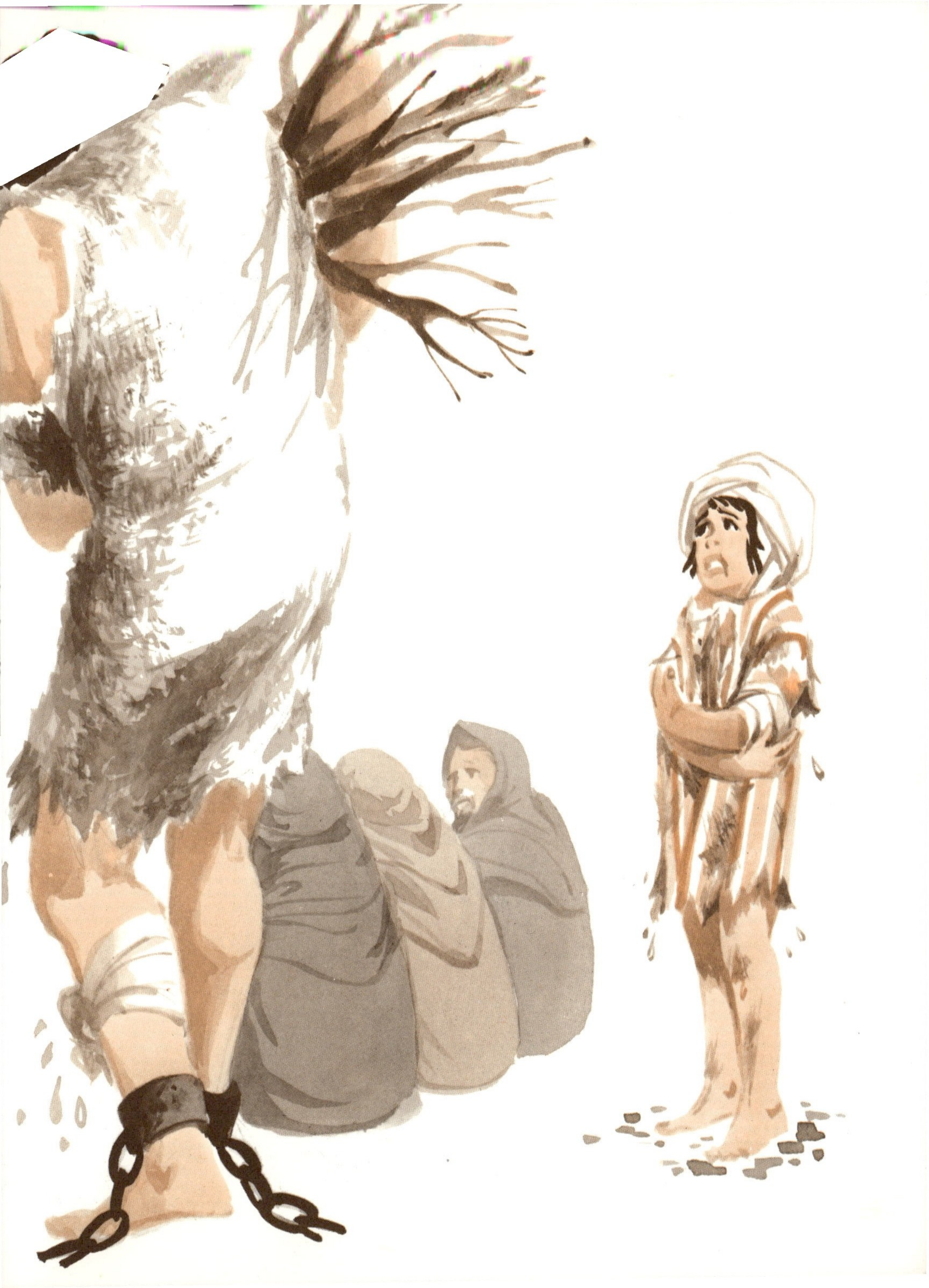

Suddenly Julie yelled,
    "Paul, drop the wood!"
But Paul stood there
        wondering why;
Then out of the wood
    shot the head of a snake
With poison
        to make a man die.

The snake bit his hand; and it wouldn't let go!
Frightened, the people all said,
"This prisoner certainly must be a killer!
It's good that he soon will be dead!"

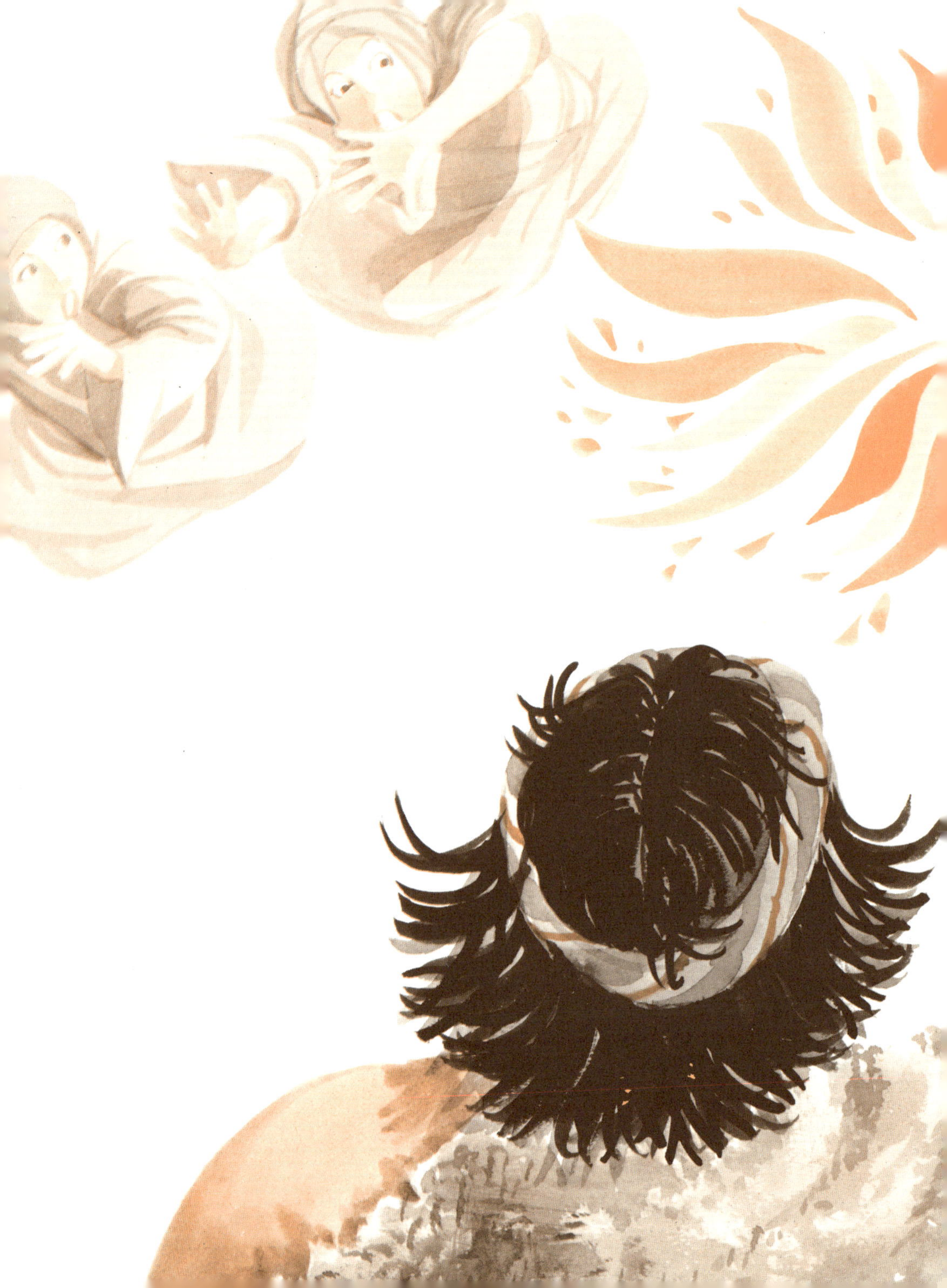

Paul shook the snake
 just a little bit harder,
And into the fire it fell.
When Paul didn't die,
 the amazed people cried,
"You must be a god; we can tell!"

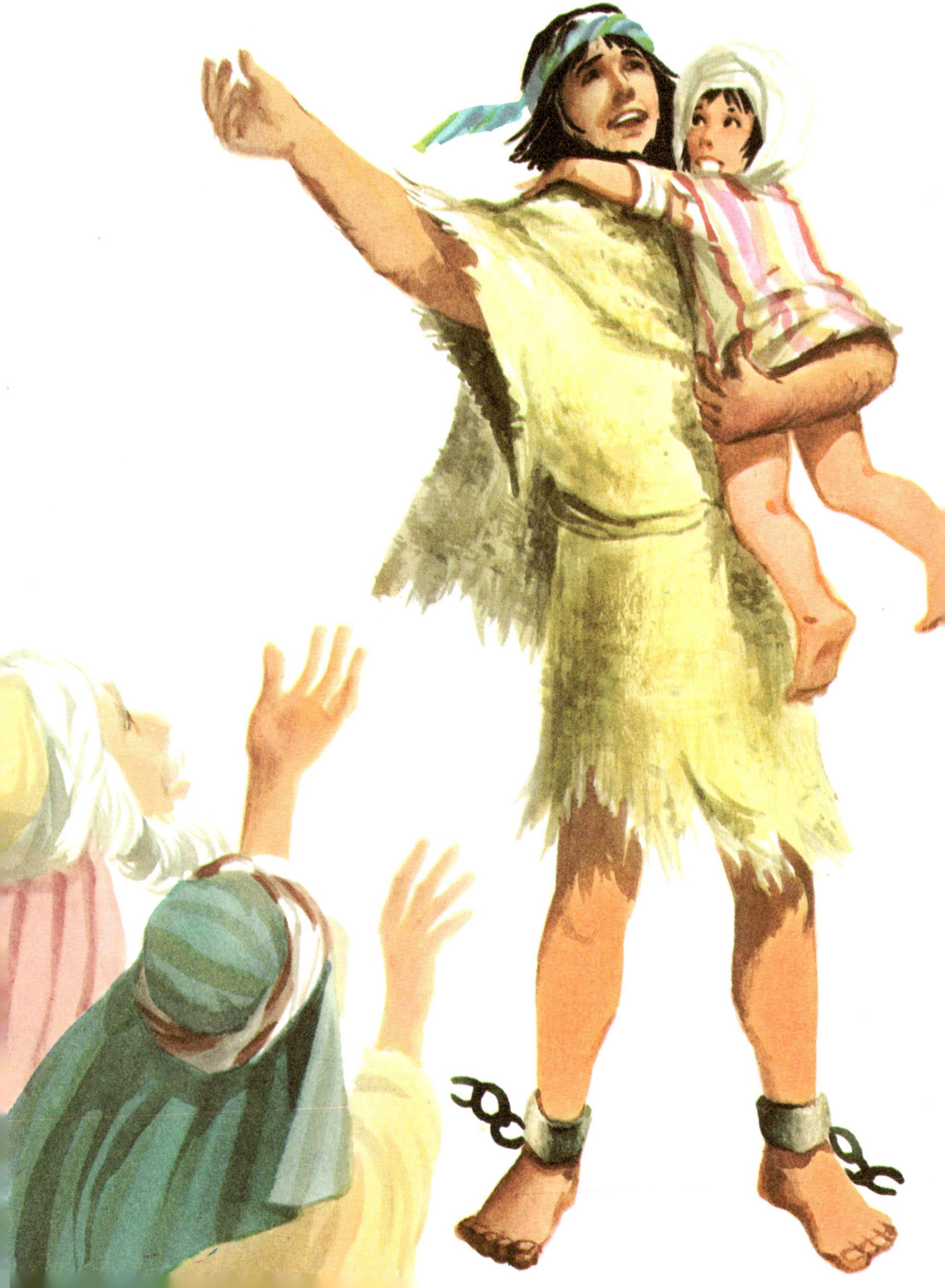

Paul picked up Julie and hugged her and said,
"Oh, no! I am only a man.
The healing was done by my God and His Son.
I'll show you His love if I can."

So, many folks living there came up to Paul,
Children and women and men.
They told him, "We all have some loved one
　　who's ill.
Can you help them get better again?"

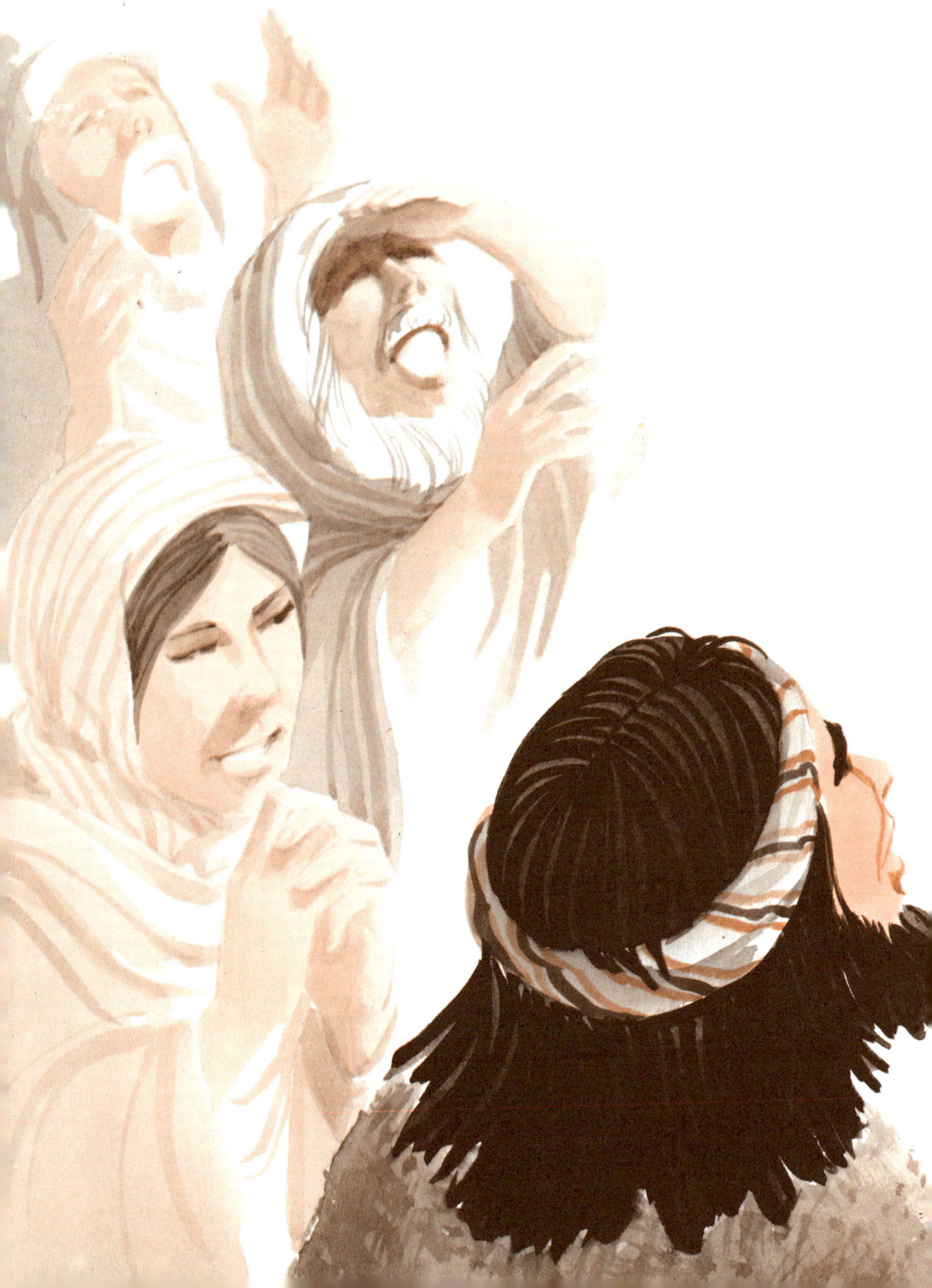

"Father in heaven," Paul cried out aloud,
"Please show them Your kindness, I pray."
Then all of the people were happy because
God healed them all right away.

Julie said, "Paul is a prisoner still.
That we all plainly can see.
But God's love has freed him
　　　　　inside where it counts,
And so he helps others be free."

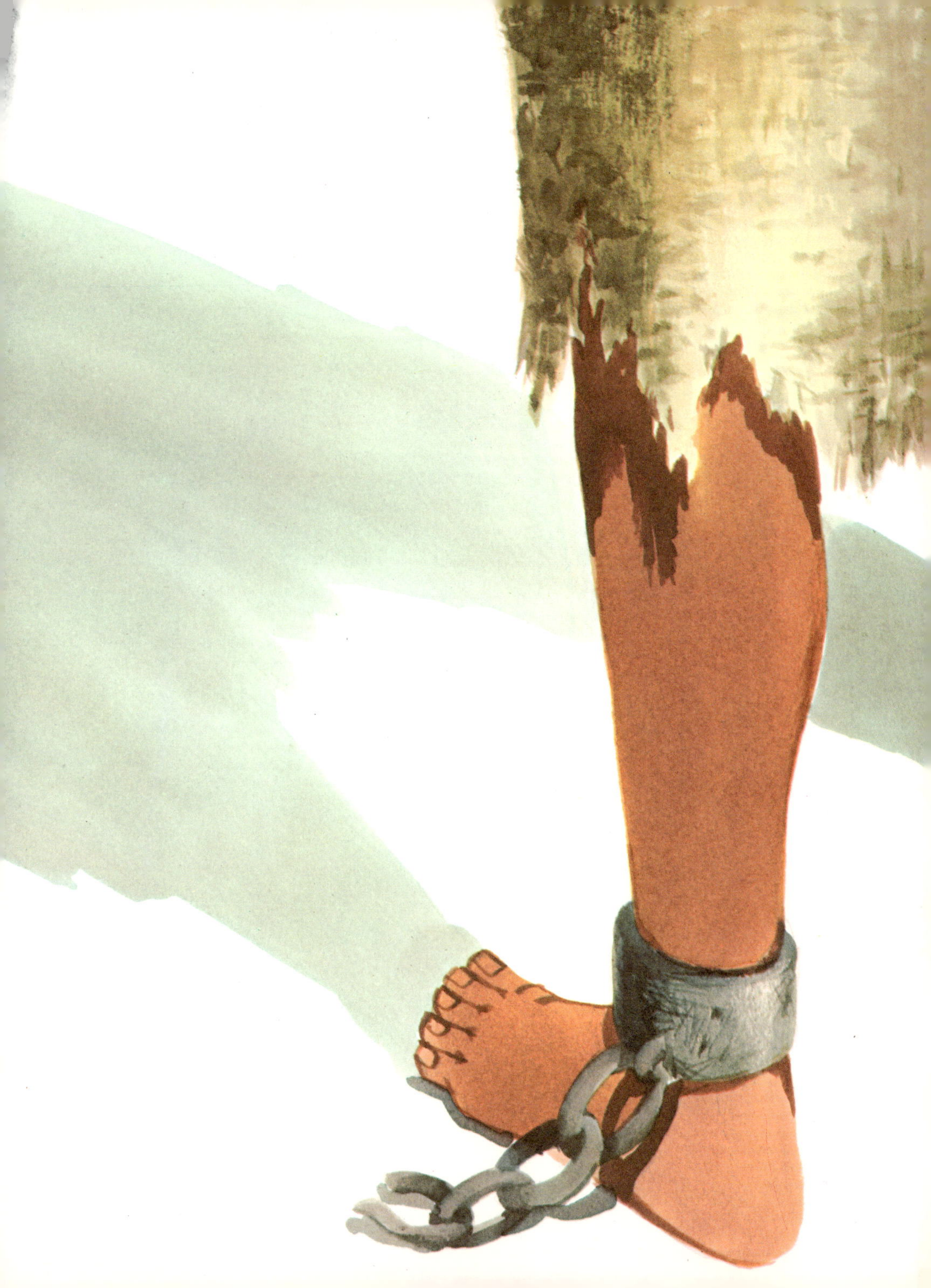

DEAR PARENTS:

Julie is a fictional character, but the story of Paul, the shipwreck, and the subsequent events on the island really happened and is recorded with explicit detail in Acts 27 and 28.

The Prisoner Who Freed Others is the story of a girl away from home for the first time. Through her contact with Paul, Julie learns that people need people and that people together need God. And she learns that because of the death and resurrection of God's Son, Jesus, we are sure of God's loving protection.

After reading this story to your child, you might mention that Paul was a real person who spent much of his adult life helping people and showing them God's love. He wrote much of the New Testament, which helps us learn more about God's love.

Help your child discover the various people in his life who show him God's love and who help him in his everyday living — parents, neighbors, older brothers and sisters, teachers, and the like. In what ways can he thank God and these people?

THE EDITOR